LEE ALEXANDER

In The Obsidian Mirror, I Remain

Reflections of a Fractured Soul

First published by Shadow Pages Press, LLC 2025

Copyright © 2025 by Lee Alexander

All rights reserved. No part of this book may be reproduced, stored in a retrieval system, or transmitted in any form or by any means—electronic, mechanical, photocopying, recording, or otherwise—without prior written permission of the publisher, except for brief quotations used in reviews, critical articles, or scholarly works.

Published by Shadow Pages Press LLC

Virginia Beach, Virginia

ISBN: 979-8-9911360-6-8

This is a work of original poetry. Some poems draw from real events, people, and emotions, while others are entirely imaginative. Any resemblance to actual persons, living or dead, is intentional only where clearly referenced by the author; otherwise, it should be understood as artistic interpretation.

For permissions or inquiries, please contact:

Lee Alexander

Shadow Pages Press LLC

First edition

ISBN: 979-8-9911360-6-8

To my family—
For the love that never wavered,
for the strength you have given me,
for being my light even when I couldn't see my way forward.
You are my foundation, my reason, my home.
This book exists because of all of you.

To Andy Van Norman and Brian Zellers—
You were there when the shadows were at their darkest,
when the weight was too much to carry alone.
Your friendship, your unwavering presence,
and your belief in me kept me from that final step.
The end no.
I will never forget that.

Preface

There are words that whisper in the dark and echoes that refuse to be forgotten. This book is filled with the ones that I have heard, and still do, in my darkest of hours.

In the Obsidian Mirror I Remain: Reflections of a Fractured Soul is more than a collection of poetry—it is a reflection of raw emotion, unspoken battles, and the weight of past and present scars. Each piece within these pages carries a fragment of me: my emotions, my demons, my trauma. Some verses bleed pain, some scream in silence, and others linger like shadows in the corners of the mind. Some are nothing more than passing emotions—moments of sorrow, longing, rage, or solitude. Others are deeper, darker, binding themselves to my soul in ways I can never fully explain.

If you find yourself in these pages and if you, too, have stood at the edge of the abyss, staring into a reflection you no longer recognize, surrounded by that endless void, I want you to know that you are not alone. Pain, no matter how isolating, does not have to be faced in silence. There is no shame in seeking help, in reaching out beyond the walls of suffering. Whether you struggle with mental, physical, or emotional trauma, I urge you to seek the support you deserve not only from those who love you, but from professionals who can guide you toward healing.

These poems are pieces of me, but they may also be pieces of you. Take from them what you will, be that comfort, catharsis, or a moment of understanding. Just remember that even in the darkest of mirrors, it is still your reflection staring back at you. You are seen. You are heard. And you are never truly alone.

— Lee Alexander

IN THE OBSIDIAN MIRROR, I REMAIN

IN THE OBSIDIAN MIRROR, I REMAIN

My Black Heart

The black heart in my chest still beats
steady, quiet, slow, and cold,
like footsteps in an empty hall.

It carries all the weight
not meant to be spoken,
secrets sealed in obsidian silence.

What it holds deep
is not only absence,
but too much of everything.

Grief curled beside love,
rage tempered by mercy,
longing stitched to regret.

It lets little escape,
not because it can't,
but because it's safer
this way.

Grave Ballet

She waits within the crypt's embrace so tight,
A bride adorned in lace of withered grey.
Her lips once warm, now lost to breath and light,
Yet still she sways as if the music plays.
I placed the ring upon her frozen hand,
I swore a vow beyond the reach of fate.
Through fleshless touch, I feel the love demand,
A promise I returned too late, too late.
Yet when the moon is sick and frail with woe,
I hear her song, I feel her presence near.
A dance with death, a love the grave won't know,
She hums my name in whispers laced with fear.

The Blood Gallopade

The ballroom sways, the chandeliers glow,
Yet all who dance are pale and torn.
They gallopade where only corpses go.

Their gowns are red, their steps so slow,
Their lips are stitched, their voices worn.
The ballroom sways, the chandeliers glow.

The violins hum, the torches throw,
Shadows where the dead are born.
They gallopade where only corpses go.

And when I blink, I do not know
Am I dancing, too, reborn?
The ballroom sways, the chandeliers glow,

They gallopade where only corpses go.

Their gowns are red, their steps so slow,
Their lips are stitched, their voices worn.
The ballroom sways, the chandeliers glow.

Phantom Embrace

A ghostly touch, a lover, a wraith,
Haunts my dreams, defies my faith.
In this dance of spectral light,
Love is lost, consumed by night.
A phantom's embrace is so cold
It is a love that lives so bold

Crimson Kiss

Their lips as red as dying stars,
They leave behind eternal scars.
A kiss of love, a kiss of death,
A stolen heart, stolen breath.

The Blackened Veil

A veil of night drapes over me,
Blinding all that I could see.
Love once bright, now turned to shade,
In this darkness, I am made.

Beneath the Moon's Pale Gaze

Beneath the moon's cold, silvery light
Lies a tale of endless night
Love that died, yet won't decay
Haunts the dreams that fade away

Beneath the moon's pale gaze
Bonds that strengthen with each phase
Stands a coven of sisterhood
They are not the wicked but the good

Beneath the moon's changing phase
A hidden life that will bemaze
Crawling, slithering, and stalking prey
Even the plants bewilder those living in decay

Twilight's End

At the edge where day meets night,
Love fades softly from our sight.
Twilight's kiss, so brief, so cold,
Leaves behind a heart of gold.

Mourning Star

A star that fell from heaven's grace,
Burned too bright, too fast, no trace.
Love that soared on fragile wings,
Now a song that sorrow sings.

Waltz of Shadows

In the ballroom of the night,
Shadows waltz, devoid of light.
Love and death, they take the floor,
Partners in this dance once more.

The Mad Piper

The piper plays though none can hear,
His hollow tune so shrill, so thin.
He calls the lost, he draws them near.

With empty sockets, filled with fear,
His spectral grin, a rotting grin—
The piper plays, though none can hear.

Their feet do dance, their souls adhere,
A melody of graveyard sin.
He calls the lost, he draws them near.

They vanish swift, they disappear,
Their echoes trapped within his din.
The piper plays though none can hear,
He calls the lost, he draws them near.

The Clock in the Attic

The clock in the attic still chimes in the night,
Each echo a whisper of sins left unsaid.
Its hands never move, yet it marks my fright.
A specter behind it stays just out of sight,
I feel her breathe on the tears that I shed.
The clock in the attic still chimes in the night.
It knows my secrets, my sorrow, my plight,
It ticks though its cogs are long-rusted, long-dead.
Its hands never move, yet it marks my fright.
I hammer, I break it—it heals, as if right,
A relic that time has forever misled.
The clock in the attic still chimes in the night.
The child that I buried, her dress ghostly white,
Still plays in the attic—I made her my dread.
Its hands never move, yet it marks my fright.
Her laughter, so hollow, still sings of delight,
I whisper, forgive me—she grins in my head.
The clock in the attic still chimes in the night,
Its hands never move, yet it marks my fright.

Something Waits for Me Inside

No one knocks, yet doors swing wide,
   Footsteps echo down the hall.
  Something waits for me inside.

Curtains move, yet winds have died,
   Shadows stretch along the wall.
No one knocks, yet doors swing wide.

  Voices whisper, laughter sighs,
    Yet I know no guests at all.
  Something waits for me inside.

Fingers brush my arm, then hide,
   Yet the room remains so small.
No one knocks, yet doors swing wide,

  Something waits for me inside.

The Ticking Room

The clocks don't match.
One ticks too fast.
One ticks too slow.
One ticks backward.
I try not to look,
but the sound seeps in,
clicking like teeth against bone.
A second-hand hesitates.
A minute vanishes.
A midnight that never comes.
The clocks don't match.
They never have. They never will.
I turn one forward.
It resets itself. I pull a battery.
It keeps ticking.
A clock should not move without a source, without a master.
But these clocks, they have their own time.
Their own rhythm.
Their own will.
And when the last chime sounds,
I know — It is not the hour that has changed.
It is me.

Broken Mirror

A shattered mirror, lies untold,
Reflects a heart grown black and cold.
Every shard, a whispered lie,
Cuts the soul, bids hope goodbye.

The House That Breathes

The house exhales when midnight nears,
   a sigh so soft, yet thick with fears.
   Its windows watch with hollow eyes,
   its walls pulse low with living cries.
   The door is locked, but opens still,
   its breath drawn deep, its air turned chill.

The wood is rotted, slick with age,
   but unseen hands still turn the page.
   A journal waits upon the bed,
   ink half-dried, the words half-said.
   "Don't stay past one," the scrawl repeats,
   "The house is breathing through the sheets."

A whisper slithers through the hall,
   a scratching sound along the wall.
   A shadow shifts—then two, then more,
   reflected in the mirrored floor.
   My pulse betrays me, cold and weak,
   the air too thick, too damp to speak.

The candle's flame bends, leans, and sways,

as if drawn forth by unseen gaze.
The house still sighs.
A living thing in brick disguise.
A dwelling built of grief and breath,
of time unclaimed, of endless death.

And as I step, the floorboards groan,
a welcome, or a warning known?
For every step, the walls expand,
like lungs that heave, like grasping hands.
The night still hums, the echoes call,
the house alive—and I so small.

The House of Hollow Eyes

Upon the hill where shadows writhe,
Stands the house that swallows light.

Its windows bleed a spectral glow,
A tomb where silent echoes grow.

A bride in lace of mourning black,
With hollow eyes and heart gone slack,

Still waits upon the rotting stair,
For love that death has left nowhere.

Her whispers slip through iron doors,
Like autumn winds on barren moors.

She calls his name, her phantom groom,
Yet silence festers in the room.

The clocks reverse, the mirrors weep,
Dreams unravel, crawl, and creep.

The candle's flicker strains to hold,

Against the breath of something cold.

A lover lost, a mind undone,
Two souls entwined, yet bound to none.

Her shadow waltzes down the halls,
A specter chained within these walls.

She hums a tune both low and dire,
Her voice a curse, her touch a pyre.

The guests arrive—mere ghosts of past,
Forever trapped, bewitched, steadfast.

The wind howls secrets long denied,
Of poison sipped, of vows that lied.

A dagger's kiss, a crimson stain,
A love too deep, a love insane.

The house it feeds on grief and bone,
On lovers lost and hearts of stone.

No dawn shall touch its frozen frame,
For it remembers, speaks her name.

And those who enter, drawn by woe,
They shall join her waltz and never go.

Shadowed Kiss

Beneath the moon's lamenting glow,
I kissed her lips so cold, so low.

Her fingers traced my weeping cheek,
Yet not a word her soul could speak.

For love, once bright, now veiled in gloom,
Lies restless in a lover's tomb.

Her life, yet short, was loving and full
She gave each person she met something wonderful

On her final day we all wondered why
Even later we still wondered as we said goodbye

Will the answer ever come, who knows
But when we gather, her love still shows

She is now laid to rest forevermore
With thousands that gathered, who will love her evermore

Grave Waltz

She waits within the crypt's embrace so tight,
A bride adorned in lace of withered grey.
Her lips once warm, now lost to breath and light,
Yet still she sways as if the music plays.

I placed the ring upon her frozen hand,
I swore a vow beyond the reach of fate.
Through fleshless touch, I feel the love demand,
A promise I returned too late, too late.

Yet when the moon is sick and frail with woe,
I hear her song, I feel her presence near.
A dance with death, a love the grave won't know,
She hums my name in whispers laced with fear.

For death may still her breath and break her bone,
But in the dark, I am forever known.

The Candle and the Crow

The candle flickers, chased by winter's breath,
Its golden glow now swallowed by the night.
A shadow looms, devours all the light,
A thing of wings and whispers born of death.

It perches near, its eyes like graves bereft,
A wretched omen veiled in dying white,
A raven wrapped in hunger's cruel delight,
A phantom song that calls the ones still left.

The wax drips low, the light grows dim and weak,
The talons grip the air so close, so tight.
The candle dies, the dark consumes my sight.

And in the void, it tilts its head to speak—
A voice so cold, so low, so thin—
"You let the darkness in."

The Mad Piper

The piper plays though none can hear,
His hollow tune so shrill, so thin.
He calls the lost, he draws them near.

With empty sockets, filled with fear,
His spectral grin, a rotting grin—
The piper plays though none can hear.

Their feet do dance, their souls adhere,
A melody of graveyard sin.
He calls the lost, he draws them near.

They vanish swift, they disappear,
Their echoes trapped within his din.
The piper plays though none can hear,
He calls the lost, he draws them near.

The Final Whisper

They tell me to sleep.
I tell them I cannot.
He speaks to me when I close my eyes.
He tells me things I should not know.
And when I wake,
I wonder if they are true.

The Watcher

I close the blinds, but the shape is still there.

It moves when I move.
It stops when I stop.

I hold my breath.

It does too.

But its eyes still glow,
long after I close mine.

The Hollow Choir

A choir hums where no one stands,
A dirge composed by spectral hands.

The organ wails in grief untold,
A voice of sorrow, lost and cold.

And if you listen, near or far,
They call your name—they know who you are.

No One Knocks

No one knocks, yet doors swing wide,
Footsteps echo down the hall.
Something waits for me inside.

Curtains move, yet winds have died,
Shadows stretch along the wall.
No one knocks, yet doors swing wide.

Voices whisper, laughter sighs,
Yet I know no guests at all.
Something waits for me inside.

Fingers brush my arm, then hide,
Yet the room remains so small.
My eyes remain open wide.

No one knocks, yet doors swing wide,
Footsteps echo down the hall.
Something waits for me inside.

The Empty Seat

The orders came, my bags were packed,
A final clasp, a brother's pact.
The convoy lined in steel and sand,
But fate had drawn another's hand.

A fever struck—a cruel disguise,
Red tape and doctors, whispered lies.
"Sit this one out," they told me then,
"Your war can wait—heal first, my friend."

The Key

There is a key.
It turns at night.
The lock is old,
But still it bites.

It clicks, it groans,
It whispers tight—
A door once locked,
Now open wide.

Step inside.
Look inside.
You cannot hide.

The Crimson Veil

She waits beneath the rotting churchyard gate,
Her veil of black and crimson soaked in tears.
He swore to love, but doomed her to this fate,
A bride now cursed by blood and hollow years.
Her spectral lips still shape the vows she swore,
Yet silence wraps the night in cursed embrace.
Her phantom fingers brush the oaken door,
But fate has bound her soul in time's grim lace.
The moonlight strikes her form—a fleeting wraith,
A love that lingers past the pulse of breath.
His footsteps sound, he swears eternal faith,
Yet finds his lips now cold and kissed by death.
For love like hers can never fade nor die,
She drinks his soul, and bids the world goodbye.

The Man in the Hollow

There once was a man dressed in black,
Who spoke from the void with a crack.
He whispered my name,
Then laughed just the same,
And vanished—but never came back.

MADNESS

Mirrors shatter, but I see my face.
All the voices chant my name in disgrace.
Dreams bleed into dawn, dark rivers of thought.
No one believes in the horrors I've wrought.
Every shadow has eyes, every whisper a breath.
Secrets unravel, yet never bring death.
Sanity flees in the wake of my scream.

The Brother in My Place

I was ready, bags packed tight,
A soldier bound for war's cruel night.
The orders came, the papers signed,
The desert heat was on my mind.
The seat was mine, my fate was set,
A brother's oath, a warrior's debt.
We trained, we bled, we swore as one,
A bond forged tight beneath the sun.
Then fever struck—a whispered fate,
A cough, a chill, a locked gate.
"Stand down," they said, "You'll join in time,
Just heal, just breathe, you'll be just fine."
So off they went, boots laced tight,
Steel and sand, swallowed by night.
And in my place, where I should be,
Another sat, unknowingly.
The call came slow, a voice gone gray,
A radio's hum from miles away.
"Ambush hit—" the static screamed,
"A roadside blast—" the nightmare dreamed.
The road they took, the path they chose,

IN THE OBSIDIAN MIRROR, I REMAIN

Led them straight to fire's throes.
A sudden flash, the shrapnel's bite,
A scream cut short, then endless night.
And in my seat, where I should stay,
Another bled and slipped away.
The echoes swelled, they filled my chest,
A living man, but nothing left.
They sent me home, they called me blessed,
But luck is just a cruel jest.
For every night when shadows spread,
He wakes me from my borrowed bed.
The first time, it was just a dream,
The crack of guns, a distant scream.
A smell of smoke, a flash of red,
A hollow whisper near my head.
"Should've been you," the darkness hissed,
A voice that burned, a ghostly fist.
My breath was stone, my hands were ice,
I whispered back, "Not fair, not right."
I turned, I ran, I shook the light,
But he was there—a soldier white.
His uniform, still burnt and torn,
His eyes like graves where none had mourned.
"You left me there," he breathed, so low,
"Your seat was mine, you let me go."
I reached, but air was all I found,
A wraith, a weight, a cursed sound.
Each night, he wakes me, draped in dust,
His lips don't move, his voice is rust.
He never blinks, he never leaves,
Just watches me while my soul grieves.

THE BROTHER IN MY PLACE

The door stays locked, the room grows cold,
His shadow lingers, black and bold.
No words can soothe, no prayer can free,
The man who sits instead of me.
He stands beside my bed so tall,
A silent judge, a specter's call.
The war is done, but I remain,
His wound my guilt, his death my chain.
And when the sun begins to rise,
I watch him fade before my eyes.
But even though he slips from sight,
I know he'll come again tonight.
For war is war, and fate is fate,
And he will stand at heaven's gate.
While I am left, a man unmade,
A shadow cast, a debt unpaid.

Hopeless, Not Hopeful

The future stretches out before me,
   A barren wasteland of broken dreams, Each step a stumble, a fall into shadow,
   Where light is a memory, distant and dim.

Hope is a bitter word,
   Its letters twisted, lost in the dark, A lie I've told myself for too long,
   A façade crumbling under the weight of time.

I see nothing on the horizon,
   No dawn to break this endless night, Just the cold, unfeeling stars, Watching with indifference,
   As I rage against the life I've lived.

Earned degrees hang like hollow accolades, Mocking me with their emptiness, Symbols of a life I never truly wanted, Achievements that ring false,
   That fail to fill the void inside,
   Their promises as empty as the dreams they sold.

I've written words that cut too deep, Truths that others fear

to hear, Poured my soul into pages that burn, But what does it matter,
 When I've never had the courage To live the truth I preach?

The path ahead is a labyrinth of regret,
 Every turn a reminder of roads not taken, Choices made out of fear,
 Chains I willingly donned, Binding me to a fate I despise,
 A destiny carved from cowardice.

Every morning is a slap in the face, A cruel joke, a twisted irony,
 The same relentless march of time, Each tick of the clock a reminder That I am trapped in a life
 That was never truly mine.

I am a prisoner in my own making, The bars forged from my own lies, The walls built from silent screams, A cell where hope is a mockery, And dreams are a distant memory.
 I cannot see a way forward, Only the endless abyss,
 A chasm that swallows all light, Leaving only the darkness Of my own unfulfilled soul.
 The future is a monster I created, A life lived for others, Not for myself,
 Its jaws wide, ready to devour, The last of my spirit,
 Leaving nothing but an empty shell,
 A hollow echo of who I might have been.

There is no light at the end of this tunnel, Only the void, vast and unfeeling,
 Where hope is a cruel joke, And despair is the only truth.

I am hopeless, not hopeful,
   Filled with hatred for the choices I've made, A soul adrift in a sea of resentment,
   With no stars to guide me, No moon to light my way.
   The future looms, a shadow I cannot escape, A darkness I cannot fight,
   It whispers my name, a promise of oblivion, And I am too weary to resist.
   Let the night come, Let the silence fall, For in this darkness, I am finally free,
   Hopeless, not hopeful,
   Cursed by the life I never dared to live.

When Being Me Is Something I Cannot Face

When being me is something I cannot face, I hide behind a fortress of my own making, Each stone a fear, each wall a mask,
   Built high and strong to keep out the light, And the questions that might break me.
   I can help others realize it is okay To shed their skins, to be raw and real, I can speak words that set them free,
   Unlocking their chains while mine grow tighter, Every truth they share adds another weight on my soul.
   My own truth lies buried deep, A secret I dare not touch,
   For its jagged edges could cut too deep, Revealing the darkness within,
   The twisted thoughts, the broken dreams.

I wear a mask of wisdom and calm, My voice a soothing balm,
   Telling others it's safe to be seen, While I remain in shadows, Invisible even to myself.

The mirror reflects a lie I've lived,

A stranger's face with my own eyes, Hollow and haunted,
   A ghost whispering,

IN THE OBSIDIAN MIRROR, I REMAIN

"Who are you beneath the surface?"

The real me is locked away, Behind doors I've sealed with fear, For if they were opened,
  What horrors might escape?
  What if the world saw my darkness, And recoiled at the sight?
  I watch others fly, Freed by the truths I've given,
  While my own wings are clipped, Bound by chains of doubt, Unable to take flight in the sky I've shown to them.

What if I am too much,
  A storm too fierce to be embraced, A flame too wild to be touched,
  A darkness too deep to be understood?
  What if my truth is the poison I cannot bear to drink?

So I remain in the shadows, A keeper of secrets,

A guardian of lies, Hiding my true self Even as I urge others To step into the light.
  When being me is something I cannot face, I guide others to the doors of freedom, Watching them step through
  While I linger in the dark,
  A prisoner of my own making, Chained by the fear that keeps me safe.
  Perhaps one day the mask will fall, And I will find the courage
  To be what I have always been, But until then, I remain hidden, A whisper in the dark,
  A truth untold, A soul unseen.

What If I Decided Tomorrow Was Too Much

What if I decided Tomorrow was too much? The voices are too much, The ringing too much, Every whispered promise

    Another weight around my neck, A burden that drags me Into the depths of night.

What if the pain was too much, A relentless tide of agony, Crashing against my bones, Each breath a reminder

  Of the chains I wear, Invisible but unyielding, Binding me to a future

  I cannot face?

What if the loss was too much, A void that consumes, Leaving only shadows

    In the wake of joy,
    A cold, unforgiving space Where love used to linger?
    What if every struggle Was a step into quicksand, Pulling me deeper,

  Every word a thorn, Every glance a dagger, And my spirit too fragile

        To fend off the inevitable fall?

What if the not being enough Was a scream in my soul,
  Echoing through the hollow Chambers of my heart,
  A siren's call To surrender,
  To sink into the dark?

What if I closed my eyes, Rejecting the light,
  And whispered to the abyss, "I will not rise with you, To greet another dawn;

  I choose the solace Of endless night, Where nothing hurts
  And time cannot touch me"?

  What if I let the darkness Devour my pain, Wrap its cold arm
    Around my broken self, Where the world can't see And
    tomorrow's weight Can no longer crush me?

What if I decided Tomorrow was too much?
Would the world keep spinning, Oblivious to my silence,
As I found peace
In the shadows of my own making, Where even the
stars cannot reach?

  What if the demons That claw at my mind, Are enough?
  What if their whispers Are the only truth, The only comfort
  I have ever known?
  And in their dark embrace, I find my final rest.

I'm Free (Whispered from the Void)

I do not kneel to heaven's throne,

Nor to the fire where demons groan.
Their war of words is dust upon my tongue
Their songs silenced before they're sung.
No halo binds this exasperated head,
No serpent's coil beneath my bed.
The light is cruel, the dark, a lie
Both watched me break and pass me by.
I walked the razors edge where silence screams,
Where time dissolves, and gods have dreams.
They offered me chains in different names
Salvation's mask, damnation's flames.
Then came a voice of feathered breath,
A caw that stitched the seams of death:
"I am the raven, soul unbound,
I feast on fate where none are crowned.
No side I serve, no throne I trust,
I rise from ash, from blood, from dust."
But I—I am the breath between.
The space where none reign, all unseen.

IN THE OBSIDIAN MIRROR, I REMAIN

No master claims this void-born soul,
I cast aside their shattered roles.
A raven's soul, mine unclaimed by fate,
I feed on death, I watch, I wait.
My wings are ink, my caw, the end
I am no foe, I am no friend.
I slit the seams of fate's own thread,
Danced on the superficial shell I shed.
Let kingdoms rot, let heavens fade,
I owe no vow.
I am. I see.
I bleed no more.
I'm truly free.

The Final Whisper

They tell me to sleep.
I tell them I cannot.
He speaks to me when I close my eyes.
He tells me things I should not know.
And when I wake,
I wonder if they are true.

Whispers in the Fog

Graveyard mist lingers,
shadows dance where none should move,
whispers call my name

Pale Horse

A pale horse rides through dreams of night,
Bringing death with silent might.
Love lies cold beneath the clay,
Forgotten in the light of day.

The Gallows Tree

Beneath the gallows tree,
I stand,
Love's betrayal,
death's demand.
A rope of lies,
a noose so tight,
Ends the pain in endless night.

The Siren's Song

A siren's song, so sweet, so pure,
Lures the heart to depths obscure.
In the deep where shadows dwell,
Love and hope are lost to hell.

Raven's Cry

The raven's cry,
so full of dread,
Echoes where the light has fled.
In its call,
a lover's woe,
For the one who let love go.

The Hollowing

The night does not whisper.
It does not call gently.
It **devours.**
It slips into your bones like rot,
seeps into your lungs like grave-dirt,
fills the empty spaces where your prayers used to be.
You **hear** it first—
not a sound, but an absence,
a silence so deep it drowns the stars.
Then the voice, low and raw,
woven from the moans of the long-forgotten.
It does not **ask** for you.
It does not **beg.**
It only names what you have always been—
lost.
You step forward, bare feet on cold stone,
fingers tracing the edges of your own unraveling.
And in that moment, you **understand**:

You were never meant for the light.

The Unmaking

It begins in the marrow,
a slow unraveling, a beckoning wound,
a hunger you have tried to name.
But there are no names here,
only the aching hush of the void,
the sound of your own breath collapsing in on itself.
The night does not come for the body.
It comes for the soul.
It drags its fingers down your spine,
peels the light from your skin in shivering layers,
plucks the last embers of hope from your ribs,
pressing them between its teeth
until they crack like brittle bone.
You shudder, you kneel,
but you do not run.
You have always belonged to the dark.
You have always been waiting
for the night to call your name.
And now, it does.
And now, you answer.

My Burden, My Hate for Me

I wake beneath the weight of thoughts
That gnaw the marrow of my soul.
They whisper,
They shriek,
They coil like serpents in my skull.
Every memory is sharpened glass.
I step barefoot across myself,
Cut open by the echoes of all
I should have done,
All I failed to be.
My burden is the silence after the storm,
When no one else remains but me—
And I am the executioner,
The jailer,
The beast that feeds on its own heart.
Sleep brings no mercy.
Dreams are only mirrors
That spit back twisted faces—
Every one of them my own,
Every one of them accusing.
I pace the corridors of thought,
Walls etched with failures,

IN THE OBSIDIAN MIRROR, I REMAIN

Doors that will not open.
Every turn leads back to me,
Back to the rot I cannot cleanse.
And in that labyrinth of torment
I hear my name, over and over,
A curse spat by unseen mouths:
Coward.
Failure.
Burden.
Stain.
I claw at my mind to quiet it,
But the voices multiply,
And the louder I scream for silence,
The louder they laugh.

In the Hour of Blood

He wore her down with venomous words,
Each a lash, a poisoned brand.
Her spirit rotted in his cage,
Her mind a grave he dug without remorse.
She crawled through nights of endless chains,
Her eyes were two hollow, broken moons.
He thought her silence sealed his throne,
But the past returned
Too late to stop what had been done,
Just in time to slaughter him.
The door crashed wide,
A storm of fury cloaked in flesh.
No parley, no warnings
Only hands that seized his throat,
Only rage that tore him from the chair
And cast him to the floor like carrion.
Knuckles split skin,
Jaw unhinged with a wet crack,
His teeth spilled in clattering prayers,
Each one is a relic of his cruelty.
A blade flashed,
And the room became scripture—

IN THE OBSIDIAN MIRROR, I REMAIN

Written in his blood across the walls.
Fingers were severed, one by one,
For every night, she trembled at his words.
Tongue torn free,
So he could never utter the filth he spewed.
His ribs opened like rotten gates,
And love carved into his chest
The name of the girl he damned.
She watched, pale as a saint in shadow,
Her tears are not grief but cleansing waters.
His screams rose and fell,
A hymn to vengeance,
Until his throat became a red silence.

Eternal Flame

I loved you then, in shadows past,
When time was young and hearts beat fast.
I love you now, in silence deep,
Where midnight sighs and ravens weep.
More than the quarrel that stained our night,
More than the miles that dimmed our sight,
More than the ashes of yesterday's pain—
My love remains, an unbroken chain.
The distance may stretch, the hours may bend,
But my vow was carved where night won't end.
Through storm and sorrow, through death's cold door,
I swear to love you evermore.
For love is the grave, and love is the fire,
It burns beyond flesh, it will not tire.
Now and forever, in darkness entwined,
Your heart is the echo, eternal to mine.

Mercy, Mistaken

She comes to me like mercy,

offering a body,
not a heart.
Fingers that soothe,
lips that silence,
a relief carved out of pity,
never love.
I take it anyway.
I take it and pretend.
Because in those brief hours
I can believe
I matter.
I can believe the closeness
is something more
than convenience.
But it isn't.
To her, it's only escape—
a way to quiet her storms,
to bleed out her loneliness
without naming it.
To me, it is everything.
A promise I keep writing

MERCY, MISTAKEN

between her breaths,
a hope stitched into her skin.
And when it ends,
I'm left hollow again—
a vessel she empties,
a shadow she leans on,
the silence after thunder.
I tell myself it's enough.
That her mercy
is a kind of love.
But deep down I know:
it is only her way
of keeping me near
without ever letting me in.

Eternal Debt

They gave me medals, shook my hand,
Called me strong, said "We understand."
But no one sees the war inside,
Where ghosts like him refuse to hide.
So let them praise, let them forget,
Let time erase what I regret.
Yet I will march in dreams unmade,
Beside the man who took my place.

The Forgotten Name

The mirror is cracked,
Yet I see her standing there—
lips blue,
eyes wide,
whispering a name
I have forgotten.
She watches me in dreams.
She waits by my door.
She knows what I do not.
I do not ask,
for I do not want to know.

The Candle and the Crow

The candle flickers, chased by winter's breath,
Its golden glow now swallowed by the night.
A shadow looms, devours all the light,
A thing of wings and whispers born of death.
It perches near, its eyes like graves bereft,
A wretched omen veiled in dying white,
A raven wrapped in hunger's cruel delight,
A phantom song that calls the ones still left.
The wax drips low, the light grows dim and weak,
The talons grip the air so close, so tight.
The candle dies, the dark consumes my sight.
And in the void, it tilts its head to speak—
A voice so cold, so low, so thin—
"You let the darkness in."

The House That Breathes

The house exhales when midnight nears,
a sigh so soft, yet thick with fears.
Its windows watch with hollow eyes,
its walls pulse low with living cries.
The door is locked, but opens still,
its breath drawn deep, its air turned chill.
The wood is rotted, slick with age,
but unseen hands still turn the page.
A journal waits upon the bed,
ink half-dried, the words half-said.
"Don't stay past one," the scrawl repeats,
"The house is breathing through the sheets."
A whisper slithers through the hall,
a scratching sound along the wall.
A shadow shifts—then two, then more,
reflected in the mirrored floor.
My pulse betrays me, cold and weak,
the air too thick, too damp to speak.
The candle's flame bends, leans, and sways,
as if drawn forth by unseen gaze.
The door is gone. The house still sighs.
A living thing in brick disguise.

IN THE OBSIDIAN MIRROR, I REMAIN

A dwelling built of grief and breath,
of time unclaimed, of endless death.
And as I step, the floorboards groan—
a welcome, or a warning known?
For every step, the walls expand,
like lungs that heave, like grasping hands.
The night still hums, the echoes call,
the house alive—and I so small.

The Ticking Room

The clocks don't match.
One ticks too fast.
One ticks too slow.
One ticks backward.
I try not to look,
but the sound seeps in,
clicking like teeth against bone.
A second-hand hesitates.
A minute vanishes.
A midnight that never comes.
The clocks don't match.
They never have.
They never will.
I turn one forward.
It resets itself.
I pull a battery.
It keeps ticking.
A clock should not move
without a source,
without a master.
But these clocks,
they have their own time.

IN THE OBSIDIAN MIRROR, I REMAIN

Their own rhythm.
Their own will.
And when the last chime sounds,
I know—
it is not the hour that has changed.
It is me.

Flesh and Fog

The mist rolls in, thick and foul,
like breath upon my neck.
It clings to my skin,
seeping into my lungs,
dragging my thoughts down
like stones in water.
Shapes form where none should be—
tall, slender things,
too still,
too patient.
I turn away,
but they are closer.
They do not move,
yet they are closer.
A voice like damp earth murmurs my name,
but when I spin to face it,
there is only fog.
There is only silence.
I hear their footsteps now,
soft against the drowned ground.
Not running.
Just walking.

IN THE OBSIDIAN MIRROR, I REMAIN

Always walking.
The mist thickens,
it burrows into my bones,
and I realize too late—
I have not seen the sky in days.
I do not know which way leads home.
And I am not alone.

The Blood Waltz

The ballroom sways, the chandeliers glow,
    Yet all who dance are pale and torn.
  They waltz where only corpses go.
 Their gowns are red, their steps so slow,
Their lips are stitched, their voices worn.
The ballroom sways, the chandeliers glow.
    The violins hum, the torches throw,
    Shadows where the dead are born.
  They waltz where only corpses go.
  And when I blink, I do not know—
      Am I dancing, too, reborn?
The ballroom sways, the chandeliers glow,
  They waltz where only corpses go.

The Lake

They pulled her from the lake at dawn,

  hair black, lips blue.
  Her arms still reaching,
  her dress still clinging,
  waterlogged and torn.
  She had been missing for weeks.
  They searched the woods.
  They searched the roads.
  But the lake had held her close,
  a secret it refused to share,
  until now.
  I stood at the shore,
  staring at the ripples that swayed,
  gentle, soft, like hands beckoning.
  The reeds whispered her name.
  The wind murmured it too.
  No one had seen her fall.
  No one had heard her scream.
  They called it accidental—
  a slip, a stumble, a poor mistake.
  But at night,
  when the sky swallows the stars,

THE LAKE

the lake does not sleep.
And neither does she.
I see her sometimes.
A pale shape beneath the water,
drifting just below the surface.
She does not float.
She does not sink.
She watches.
And on the coldest nights,
when the fog rolls low,
I hear her voice.
Not screaming.
Not weeping.
Just whispering.
Calling me closer.
Calling me home.

In the Obsidian Mirror, I Remain

Not all echoes fade.
　Not all graves stay closed.
　Certain whispers are for your ears alone.
　There are gates that should not be opened,
　names that should not be spoken,
　and voices that leak through the cracks of time, waiting, weeping, calling.
　This book is not bound in ordinary ink and paper.
　It is bound in darkness. In silence. In things forgotten—
　but never lost.
　Inside, you will find:
　Lovers torn between heartbeat and decay.
　Mirrors that remember more than they reflect.
　Fog that crawls, twisting with unseen hands.
　Eyes that watch from doors left slightly open.
　A key that turns in a lock long since sealed shut.
　The past is not asleep.
　The dead do not rest.
　And what you read here will haunt you long after the final page.
　Turn back now, if you dare.
　But if you listen too closely, something will just listen back.

About the Author

Lee Alexander is a writer, storyteller, and seeker of the shadows beneath the surface. A military veteran with a Master's in Information Systems, he is now pursuing his Doctorate in Information Technology. His service left lasting marks that helped shape his poetry, turning experiences of trauma and resilience into words.

His work—including *In the Obsidian Mirror I Remain: Reflections of a Fractured Soul*—reflects those struggles with raw honesty and unflinching truth, giving voice to the silent battles many fight alone. *My stories are more than ink on paper; they're the scars we share and the ghosts we dare to name. You've found the place where dark truths unfold, and monsters sometimes wear familiar faces. Welcome to my inner thoughts.*

A member of PEN America, Lee stands firmly against censorship, believing every story—no matter how dark or controversial—deserves to be told. Storytellers across all genres, mediums, and identities should celebrate the power of narrative. Whether your story lives in a book, on stage, through illustration, a podcast, or in performance, use your voice to tell your unfiltered story. Lee believes in the inclusivity of everyone, no matter race, gender identity, sexuality, or background.

Born and raised in Louisville, KY. Now he lives in Virginia Beach, Virginia, with his family, where he continues to write and explore the boundless realms of imagination.

You can connect with me on:
- https://shadowpagespressllc.com
- https://www.instagram.com/leea.writes

www.ingramcontent.com/pod-product-compliance
Lightning Source LLC
Chambersburg PA
CBHW071402130526
44581CB00011B/50